NAVIGATING YOUR NEW YORK

POST-DIVORCE CASE:

Modifications & Enforcement

David I. Bliven

Jacobs & Whitehall
21750 Hardy Oak Blvd
Suite 104
#51700
San Antonio, Texas 78258
www.jacobsandwhitehall.com

Ordering Information:

Quantity sales. Special discounts are available on quantity purchases by corporations, associations, and others. For details, contact the publisher at the address above.

Orders by U.S. trade bookstores and wholesalers. Please contact Jacobs & Whitehall: Tel: (888) 991-2766 or visit www.jacobsandwhitehall.com.

Printed in the United States of America

Published in 2021

ISBN: 978-1-954506-33-6

FOREWORD

While many couples who divorce never have to return to court, for others the divorce judgment is just the beginning of numerous trips back to court.

Indeed, one estimate has it that nearly $10 billion in child support is owed to custodial parents nationwide - and less than half of child support orders are actually followed[1]. Likewise, though statistics vary from state to state and year-to-year, nearly half of orders of protection are violated[2].

---

[1] https://www.cbsnews.com/news/10-billion-in-child-support-payments-going-uncollected-according-to-estimates/#:~:text=A%20U.S.%20Census%20report%20estimates,t%20receive%20anything%20at%20all.

[2] This article cited to statistics varying from 7% to 81%: http://jaapl.org/content/38/3/376#:~:text=Protection%20Orders%20and%20Violence&text=The%20reported%20rates%20of%20protection,as%20high%20as%2081.3%20percent.&text=Many%20studies%20of%20protection%20orders,and%20short%20follow%2Dup%20periods.; See this article as well, finding 44% reported violations: https://www.ncbi.nlm.nih.gov/pmc/articles/PMC1448307/.

And these are just two types of orders stemming from a Divorce case which can be modified or violated – the others include property/asset distributions, alimony/maintenance awards and custody/parental access orders. Similarly, one can be issued most of these orders in a Family Court case – in such instance orders are generally enforced or modified in the court of issuance.

This book will address general information regarding modification and enforcement of New York family law orders. This should neither be considered either an all-encompassing treatise, nor take the place of advice given by an attorney in the field. Indeed, if you find yourself the recipient of an application to modify or enforce a prior family law order – or you're seeking to file one yourself – you shouldn't hesitate to contact an attorney to set-up a consultation. Many Family Law attorneys will give free or low-cost consultations – with the proviso that one gets what one pays for.

As with my other books, I must also caution the reader against consulting with – or retaining – an attorney who doesn't specialize in Family Law. A "jack of all trades is a master of none." And when you have an important Family Law case, it's generally better to rely on a "master."

Finally, if you're seeking to enforce an order, bear in mind the Judge may order your ex-spouse or the other parent to pay the fees your attorney would otherwise assess to you - so don't hesitate to retain good, competent counsel for your case.

DISCLAIMER

This publication is intended to be used for educational purposes only. No legal advice is being given, and no attorney-client relationship is intended to be created by reading this material. The author assumes no liability for any errors or omissions or for how this book or its contents are used or interpreted, or for any consequences resulting directly or indirectly from the use of this book. For legal or any other advice, please consult an experienced attorney or the appropriate expert, who is aware of the specific facts of your case and is knowledgeable in the law in your jurisdiction.

The Law Offices of David Bliven

www.blivenlaw.net

White Plains Office
19 Court St.
Suite 206
White Plains, NY 10601
(914) 468-0968

Bronx Office
3190 Riverdale Avenue
Suite 1
Bronx, NY 10463
(718) 725-9600

TABLE OF CONTENTS

CHAPTER 1

ENFORCEMENT & MODIFICATION OF ORDERS OF PROTECTION

Proceedings to Enforce of Orders of Protection

Generally, family offense orders of protection can be enforced in one of two ways.

1. **Call the Police.** If you are granted an order of protection against someone and they violate it, you always have the option of calling the police. Reporting the violation of one or more terms of

your Order of Protection can result in the immediate arrest of the respondent.

2. **File an Enforcement Petition.** Another way to enforce an order of protection is to file an enforcement petition in Family Court[3]. An enforcement petition essentially accuses the respondent of violating your Order of Protection.

Once an enforcement petition is filed, the court schedules a trial deciding whether the respondent actually violated the order of protection. During the trial, the petitioner has the burden of proving the respondent violated the Order against them. The standard of proof they must meet depends on what sort of a case is being pursued.

---

[3] Again, even if your original order of protection is granted by the Supreme Court in your divorce case, most enforcement cases are filed in family Court. It's not technically wrong to file the application in Supreme Court – but if enforcement of that order is the order issue being brought to Court, the Supreme Court has the power to "refer" the case to Family Court (meaning transfer of the case) – and if they do it may cause the filer unnecessary time and expense.

In a Family Court case, as in many civil cases, the petitioner must prove their case according to a standard known as a "preponderance of evidence". This means the evidence they bring must convince the court it is "more likely than not" that the violation occurred.

In a case where there are criminal-like consequences (i.e., probation, fine, etc.), the petitioner needs to prove their case by the stricter standard of "clear and convincing evidence" (a/k/a "reasonable certainty"). This requires that the evidence must convince the court that it is "substantially" more provable that the violation occurred. However, if the Court is looking to incarcerate the alleged offender, then the petitioner must prove his/her case by the same standard used in criminal court – "beyond a reasonable doubt."

In these cases, if the petitioner is able to provide sufficient proof, the offender can be jailed for up to 6 months for each individual violation of the petitioner's Order of Protection. So, if a petitioner alleges that the respondent violated the Order of Protection in question multiple times, the court could theoretically sentence him/her to 6 months in jail for each and every violation.

How Soon After A Family Offense Motion Is Made In Court Will A Hearing Be Held?

Hearings are usually held within two to four months - depending on the court's backlog (as of this writing in June, 2021, the courts are still very backed-up due to the pandemic), the attorney's calendar, and pre-trial motion practice. Either side can file a pre-trial motion requesting the judge issue an order, such as a discovery order or a motion to dismiss. These motions may delay the proceedings or, in the case of dismissal, it may prevent the need for a trial in the first place. If there is a basis to dismiss a petition for failure to state the cause of action, one should pursue this with their attorney.

Is It Possible For Someone To Be Removed From Their Home Prior To A Family Offense Case Being Heard In Court?

Yes a person may be removed from the home in family offense cases, especially when the allegations involve violence and the court wants to make sure that the violence does not reoccur. The court has the power to enforce a stay away order that would effectively result in a removal of that person from the residence. If the person has no other place to go, they should immediately file an order to show cause back, before the same judge asking for modification of that order, so that it would allow them to go back into the house if there is a basis to do so.

What Happens at a Trial of an Order of Protection Enforcement case?

A trial will involve both sides testifying, presenting witnesses and other relevant evidence. Oftentimes, the parties themselves are the only witnesses to the domestic violence – and thus they are usually the only witnesses.

Nevertheless, when each party testifies (called "direct examination"), then the other side's attorney is allowed to ask them questions to challenge their version of events (this is called "cross examination"). Beyond eyewitnesses, common witnesses include experts in the field of domestic violence – as well as witnesses who may have heard or seen exculpatory or incriminating evidence regarding one of the parties.

Likewise, common forms of documentary evidence include pictures, e-mails, texts, social media posts as well as audio or video evidence. One will want to full discuss with his/her attorney what witnesses and evidence s/he wishes to present, as well as thoroughly prepare for both the direct examination as well as discuss with your attorney what questions you may wish him/her to ask the other side on cross-examination.

If you're wanting to look at a mock trial of a family offense proceeding, you may access one here: https://nysba.org/products/family-court-trial-institute-orders-of-protection-2016/.

What Penalties can a Judge Direct if the Respondent is found Guilty of Violating an Order of Protection?

There are numerous penalties a Judge can order is violated – among them are:

- Modifying or extending the original order of protection;
- Placing the respondent on probation;
- Directing respondent to complete a batterer's program, anger management, or enter into drug/alcohol rehab;
- Directing "restitution" of up to $10,000;
- Directing payment of counsel fees to the victim;
- Directing medical insurance coverage and reimbursement for any medical costs incurred by the victim as a result of the incident(s);
- Directing interim custody and/or child support;
- Incarceration of up to 6 months for each separate incident alleged & proved.

* * *

Modification of Family Offense Orders

A Modification Petition or a Petition to Terminate a Family Offense Order can be requested under a number of different circumstances. This is usually done by filing an order to show cause, along with an affidavit justifying the modification of the order of protection[4].

For instance, let's say a respondent had a "stay-away" Order of Protection entered against them by someone they live with. This type of order requires the respondent to physically stay away from the petitioner, as well as his/her home, workplace, or school. Obviously, this poses logistical issues if the petitioner and the respondent share a home.

To address those issues, the respondent may decide to file a Modification Petition to challenge the "stay-away" portion of the Order of Protection, or to amend it such that they are not barred from their home. In the same situation, if the respondent simply wants to enter the home to retrieve their belongings, they may file a Modification Petition asking for the Judge's permission to do so without violating the Order.

---

4 The form for the affidavit can be found here: https://www.nycourts.gov/LegacyPDFS/FORMS/familycourt/pdfs/GF-5d.pdf.

Another common use of Modification Petitions has to do with something called a "usual terms" order of protection. A "usual terms" order bars the respondent from committing certain standard family offenses against the petitioner. In some cases, behaviors escalate and circumstances change, and the petitioner may request a Modification Petition to add additional protections (like a no-contact provision or a stay-away provision) to their Order.

A petitioner may also ask for certain provisions to be made more specific. For instance, let's say the petitioner's original Order had a no-contact provision, but the respondent simply started using a third party to contact the petitioner instead. In that case, the petitioner may file a modification petition asking the court to change the order and bar third-party communication as well.

New York State law also provides a way for petitioners/victims of family offenses to extend the length of an order of protection. For example, if a petitioner has an Order of Protection that was entered into for one year, and they feel they need protection beyond that year, they can file a Motion to extend the Order. In most courts, this should be done via an order to show cause accompanied by an Affidavit[5] justifying the extension.

Usually, there has to be some kind of factual basis ("good cause") to extend an order of protection. When requesting an extension, the petitioner will be asked to present their reasoning for the extension, as well as any evidence. The court will hear the petitioner's case, and if they feel the petitioner has stated a good factual basis on which to extend the Order, the Judge will do so.

What Does The Court Consider When Determining Whether To Modify The Terms Of A Protection Order In New York Family Court?

When considering whether to modify the terms of a protection order, the court will be looking at a number of factors.

---

[5] The form for an Affidavit requesting extension of an order of protection may be found here: https://www.nycourts.gov/LegacyPDFS/FORMS/familycourt/pdfs/GF-10-a.pdf.

First, they will be looking at the factual basis stated as to why the Order needs to be modified. Let's use the example of the person with a "stay away" Order of Protection to illustrate this point. Let's say the respondent comes to court with a Modification Petition asking to remove the "stay away" provision in the Order of Protection against them. They may argue the "stay away" portion excludes them from their own home and should be removed on that basis.

While the Judge in this case is obliged to consider the argument and evidence presented by the respondent, they will ensure the reasoning is sound and actually justifies removing that portion of the Order. They will be especially careful if there has not yet been a trial on the issue, because there is no precedent of behavior or rulings to look back on. Indeed, the statute requires the Judge to "consider whether the order of protection is likely to achieve its purpose in the absence of [the interim] condition."

Many times, if a Judge has already excluded someone from a specific activity or area, they will be hesitant to remove that restriction. Unless the respondent can convincingly argue they will literally be out on the street if they aren't allowed back into their home, it is unlikely a Judge will lift the "stay-away" portion of the Order of Protection. Instead, the Judge will usually say the respondent's best remedy is to seek an expedited trial on the family offense issue. It is the court's responsibility to protect vulnerable people, and in this case, they often prioritize the protection of victim or alleged victim (who would've stated they do not feel safe with the respondent in the house with them).

If the court has already found the respondent was guilty of committing a family offense, their request to modify or amend the Order of Protection against them will be examined through that lens. Specifically, the court will look at the factual bases of the request, and will consider what (if anything) has changed since the Order of Protection was entered into in the first place.

For instance, if the respondent has taken steps to address their behavior and improve the situation, that will be considered. They may be able to show s/he has gone to counseling, for example, or attended a batterer's program or an anger management program. If substance abuse was an issue, they can show they have completed rehab and/or stayed clean and sober. They will then try to discern whether those changes warrant some kind of modification of the Order.

On the other hand, if a victim is petitioning the court to modify their Order of Protection, the court will still want to examine the situation so as to make sure the victim is not acting under duress, or otherwise being coerced or pressured to request the modification. If the court feels the victim is acting under duress, coercion, or pressure, then they may make a referral to the District Attorney's office and/or Child Protective Services to make sure everyone (including children, if relevant) will continue to be safe and protected.

Can Family Violence Serve As Material Change To A Standing Order Of The Court?

Domestic violence may be a material change that could serve as a basis to modify custody or visitation arrangements (see the chapters below on custody modification) - however it is usually not a basis to modify a prior order of child or spousal support. One could claim their ex-spouse or the other parent of their child or children assaulted them so badly they are unable to work. In theory, one could file a modification of spousal and/or child support, claiming the other engaged in this conduct and they are now unable to work. However, this would usually be one factors amongst many in determining whether to modify such an order (see the chapters below on modification of support orders).

CHAPTER 2

CHILD CUSTODY & VISITATION MODIFICATION PETITIONS

Child custody modification petitions are almost as common as initial petitions. Over time, things tend to change for a variety of reasons. A lot of times, people establish custody when the children are relatively young. Then, as the children age or different circumstances happen, they need to modify custody or visitation. Unfortunately, some people can never solve their initial conflicts. They just fester over time and one parent or the other petitions for sole custody.

Factors Must Be Considered In Order for the Court to Grant A Modification to a Child Custody Order in New York

The first factor the court needs to consider is whether there has been a change of circumstances since the last order was set. The second factor the petition needs to state is *why* the requested change is in the best interests of the child or children. The issue will be how they go about presenting the evidence that would match up to the best interests of the children. The other sub-factors include:

1) the original placement of the child,
2) the length of that placement,
3) the child's desires,
4) the relative fitness of the parents,
5) the quality of the home environment,
6) the parental guidance given to the child,
7) the parent's financial status,
8) his or her ability to provide for the child's emotional and intellectual development, and

9) the willingness of the parent to assure meaningful contact between the child and the other parent[6].

How Is A Substantial Change Of Circumstances Affecting The Welfare Of The Child Defined Under New York State Law?

The statute does not define a substantial change of circumstances or what constitutes "best interests." Instead, it is very much case law driven and it goes back to the original custody determination factors (https://www.blivenlaw.net/child-custody/). Among other things, the court is going to look at why you are petitioning for a change. Maybe one parent is moving far away, such that it would affect the other parent's access time. Perhaps one parent has withheld access from the other parent or has not properly cared for the children. It goes back to all of the same factors that are considered in an original

[6] *Anonymous 2011-1 v. Anonymous 2011-2*, 136 A.D.3d 946, 26 N.Y.S.3d 203 (2d Dep't 2016).

custody determination and adds which factors have now changed.

What Is The Best Interest Of The Child When Considering A Modification Of Child Custody Petition In New York?

The best interest of the child or children is not statutorily driven; it is case law driven and the consideration is based on the custody factors. Among those custody factors is the age and preferences of the children, whether there is the existence of child abuse or neglect, whether there is interference with the relationship of either parent, the quality of housing, and the financial circumstances of each parent. One major factor is willingness to encourage a relationship with the other parent. One aspect of that is withholding access; another aspect is the non-custodial parent speaking badly about the custodial parent to the children. Perhaps that needs to be considered by the court in restricting some kind of access with the non-custodial parent, if they do not stop such behavior.

Process to Petition for a Modification to a Child Custody Order

In Family Court, you would file a petition with the court[7]. In Supreme Court, you would file an order to show cause, which is a type of motion or application that usually needs to be drafted by an attorney. The court can help you draft it, if you are representing yourself, but it is usually advisable to go through an attorney. Some attorneys, especially post-pandemic, offer to help draft applications for potential clients just to get them into court, without necessarily taking on the retainer (perhaps for a reduced fee).

How Long Does It Take For A Decision To Be Made On A Petition To Modify Child Custody In New York?

The amount of time it takes for a modification decision varies with each case. You could have a determination made on the first day of court. Other

---

[7] The form for a Custody/Visitation Modification Petition is here: https://www.nycourts.gov/LegacyPDFS/FORMS/familycourt/pdfs/gf-40.pdf.

cases become contested such that a hearing or trial is necessitated. It depends on what exactly is being tried. A full-blown custody case in the greater New York City area can last a year or more, but only about 5% of cases go through to a full trial. At some point, there is a resolution reached in the vast majority of modification cases.

If Both Parents Agree To The Child Custody Modification, Will The Modification Be Automatically Approved By The Court?

The court does not necessarily have to approve a modification merely because both parties agree. For instance, if the court perceives that the resolution would put the child at risk of harm, the court can order a an investigation & report by the state agency (ACS or CPS) charged with protecting children from abuse or neglect to weigh in on the issue before a decision is made.

Will Supreme Court Or Family Court Hear The Petition To Modify A Custody Order?

If the original order was created in Supreme Court pursuant to a divorce filing, then the parties usually have the option of either going back to Supreme Court or filing in Family Court for the custody modification. If the custody or visitation is the only issue you are bringing back to court, you are probably better off going to Family Court than to Supreme Court. But if there are intertwined issues of custody and visitation and also child support and property distributions, the parties are better proceeding in Supreme Court.

How Does The Petitioning Party Prove A Substantial Change Of Circumstances When Requesting A Modification To A Child Custody Order In New York?

A change of circumstances is proven in a similar way that the original custody determination would be proven: with evidence. Especially in high conflict situations: keep a very careful paper trail!

If the non-custodial parent is deprived visitation, they need to keep a paper trail of the missed or cancelled visits. I recommend creating evidence through emails or text messages with the other parent, documenting every time your visitation was denied. The other parent may ignore that correspondence but it will seem relatively unbelievable to a Judge that the person is never getting any of your text messages or emails. One can also use programs such as "Our Family Wizard"[8] or "2 Houses"[9] to document communications with the other parent (indeed, such programs are often better at organizing such communications than mere text/e-mail chains).

You should also capture your understanding of important discussions or exchange of documents. The e-mails should confirm the substance of any conversation you had with the other parent, or your attempts to contact him/her regarding visits (including confirming any messages left for him/her). The email should request that s/he respond, and specifically request that "if anything I have stated in this letter is incorrect, please return correspondence."

---

[8] https://www.ourfamilywizard.com/.

[9] https://www.2houses.com/en/.

You should minimize your utilization of relatives/babysitters to care for the child. It will ultimately look bad to the Judge if, on even some of your access time, your child is spending a significant amount of time away from you. The access time is meant to be quality time shared between you and the child.

Furthermore, log into the journal all contacts with your child, all negative contacts with the other parent, as well as contacts with the child's school, doctors, etc. Also, start thinking of any family members, teachers, clergy, etc. who would make good witnesses for trial.

If an emergency arises and/or you wish to file an application to advance the court date (based on an urgent need), then you have the ability to file an order to show cause. Bear in mind it's in the discretion of the court to determine whether a genuine emergency/urgency exists. To file an order to show cause, you'll need to schedule an appointment with your attorney to complete an affidavit which must accompany same.

You're should review your Facebook, Twitter, e-mail, or other social networking pages you may keep on the internet for content which may portray you in a bad light. As an example, don't post pictures of you out partying at 6 a.m. You generally have a duty to preserve evidence, which includes electronically stored information, and therefore you should not erase or delete such evidence even if you think it's harmful. Instead, you should bring it to the attention of your attorney as you can discuss with him/her what, if anything, should be done.

To the degree the other parent harasses, threatens, intimidates or otherwise relates inappropriate comments to you, then start taping all phone conversations with him/her, including any messages left for you. You may use the "voice recorder" or "voice memo" app on your cell phone for this purpose (or a hand-held recorder). You should refrain, however, from taping any of the child's conversations.

Additionally, if you are aware of, or suspect, that the other parent, or someone largely responsible for the child's care has abused or neglected the child, or that the child is in imminent danger of being abused or neglected, you should (at the least) contact your attorney immediately. You should also, under such circumstances, consider contacting the police and/or the Statewide Central Register of Suspected Child Maltreatment (800-342-3720). Prior to contacting the police and/or Statewide Central Register, however, you should generally speak with your attorney first about the situation (unless the child's life is in imminent danger). Besides physical or sexual abuse, child neglect *may* consist of the following types of conduct (and may also address present circumstances and/or such conduct in the recent past): excessive corporal punishment, persistent and/or serious acts of domestic violence, repeated drug/alcohol abuse, mental illness, leaving young children unattended or without adequate guardianship and/or not providing a child with adequate food, shelter, clothing, education or medical care.

I also recommend keeping an event timeline – see **Appendix A** for an example.

Dangers of Petitioning for Custody/Visitation Modification

If one parent petitions for a custody modification, the other parent may also cross-petition and ask for changes which benefit them. The court can consider both petitions but one cannot end up worse off than they began on their own application (unless the Judge grants the cross-petition). For example, if a custodial parent files a petition to change some aspect of decision-making, the Judge cannot decide to switch physical custody of the child to the other parent in the absence of a cross-petition from the other parent. If the petitioning parent has not satisfied their case, the only remedy of the Judge is to dismiss their application. If there is a wide disparity of income, the more-monied parent could also sustain an award of counsel fees to the less-monied parent.

Can A Modification To A Child Custody Or Visitation Order Ever Be Challenged By The Other Party? What Are Grounds For Appeal?

Just because one parent files a custody modification application does not mean the other parent cannot challenge the basis under which they are asking for the modification. As a general rule, the court would need to hold a hearing or trial before making a determination. There are some exceptions to this general rule, but that is certainly the preference before making any kind of important change - especially an access change or switching custody from one parent to another.

Either parent who disagrees with the Judge's determination can file an appeal. There is no legal standard they must satisfy before they file the appeal – if one disagrees with the Judge's determination, one simply files a "notice of appeal.[10]" Whether the appellate court rules in their favor a completely different matter. The usual standard is whether the appellate court believes the trial court has committed an "abuse of discretion." Trial Judges have a wide latitude of discretion in making determinations on

---

10 The form for a notice of appeal may be found here: https://www.nycourts.gov/courts/AD2/forms/noticeofappeal.pdf. However, one should consult with the Court – or better yet with an attorney – to ensure one is submitting all necessary forms for the appeal.

custody. However, roughly 20% of appeals are satisfied - meaning the appellate court either reverses the trial court or determines there are some issues which need clarification (and thus send the case back to the trial court for a further hearing).

What Evidence Can A Parent Provide To Challenge The Petition To Modify A Custody Order?

If a parent alleges there is abuse or neglect going on, for example, then they have to show actual evidence of same. For example, a doctor may make a report of abuse or neglect. Children can also make disclosures to teachers, guidance counselors, or therapists and you can bring that into the case as evidence.

Evidence can also take the form of testimony - both of the parties & witnesses. One can seek to present videos, audios, e-mails/texts/social media post, pictures as well as experts and rebuttal witnesses.

Is It Always Necessary To Have A Family Law Attorney Experienced In Handling Custody Modifications To Handle My Case?

While an attorney is not always necessary, it is almost always beneficial. One could, in theory, handle their own case but, as the old adage says, one who represents himself has a fool for a client. If the other side has an attorney, you definitely want an attorney on your side. In New York State, if you cannot afford an attorney, you would qualify for court-assigned counsel. There is almost no excuse to be unrepresented on such an important issue. Ultimately, if you are assigned an attorney that you are not pleased with, you're always free to go out and hire your own attorney.

CHAPTER 3

ENFORCING CUSTODY/VISITATION ORDERS

If a parent isn't following custody orders in New York, your options depend on the seriousness of the order violation. If they are depriving access or a potential case of parental kidnapping (or what amounts to parental kidnapping), the matter needs to go to court immediately. In that case, your best option is to file an Order to Show Cause. If you are the custodial parent, you can also file a Writ of Habeas Corpus in conjunction with the Order to Show Cause.

This is a court order which means "return of the body" in Latin. It essentially compels the other parent to return the child immediately.

If the matter is less serious than deprivation of access or potential parental kidnapping, your best option is to issue a Default Notice Letter. This specifies the violation and either asks the other party to immediately remedy the violation or to immediately contact the issuer to negotiate a remedy. If the issue has not been remedied and no effort has been made to come to a resolution within a certain number of days, you may be able to follow up by filing a Violation of Enforcement Petition. This petition, often filed in family court, is usually most successful if there is a pattern of violations by the offending parent.

What Happens If The Custodial Parent Violates A Visitation Order In New York?

If the custodial parent fails to produce a child for a scheduled visit, the non-custodial parent should immediately ask why in an email or a text. This documents the violation, but also allows for the possibility that there really is an innocent reason - like the child being sick or the two of them getting stuck in traffic. If there really was a legitimate reason why the custodial parent didn't bring the child to the right place at the right time, the non-custodial parent should simply be given makeup time at a later date.

If there is a pattern of missed visits with no acceptable explanation, then the non-custodial parent should file an enforcement action in court. Contrary to popular belief, they should actually file that sort of order sooner rather than later. They should not wait for the violations to stack up for many months, because at that point a Judge may question why they waited so long to bring that issue back to court.

How Can I Prove That A Custody Or Visitation Order Is Not Being Followed?

This depends on the alleged violation and the order.

For example, let's say you are the custodial parent, and your co-parent is not showing up for visits when they are supposed to. One should carefully document every violation in order to create a paper trail (or an e-trail, as the case may be). You can do this by sending an email or text message[11] every time your co-parent violates the order, describing exactly how, when, and where that violation took place. For instance, if your co-parent doesn't show up for a visit one evening, you can send a text like the following:

"Hey, you were supposed to show up at 6:00 PM tonight, but you didn't show up. I don't know why. You also didn't contact me beforehand. Please make sure to come to scheduled visitations, and if you are unable to do so, please make sure to contact me beforehand."

Of course, in some cases, the flipside happens. For example, let's say you're the non-custodial parent, and the custodial parent is not producing the child for visits when they are supposed to. In that case, you should also document the violations every time they happen - by text or email. Thus, if you show up to the

---

[11] In my opinion, E-mails are better than texts, texts are better than nothing. One can also rely on audios of conversations, or printouts from communication programs such as Our Family Wizard.

custodial parent's house for a scheduled 6:00 PM visit, and the child is not produced at that time, you can send a text like the following:

"Hey, you were supposed to make our child available for visitation at 6:00 PM tonight. I showed up, but the child was not there, and I don't know why. You also didn't contact me beforehand. Please make sure to bring our child to scheduled visitations, and if you are unable to do so, please make sure to contact me beforehand. In addition, please contact me as soon as possible to schedule a make-up visit."

These are just two examples of things that people can do to document violations. Documenting violations with a paper trail is always a good idea. However, you should also keep in mind that the evidence needed to successfully prove an order has been violated depends on the extent & context of the violation.

I Am Being Held In Contempt For Failing To Comply With A Child Custody Order In New York. What Does That Mean?

"Contempt of court" simply means it's been alleged that you've violated an order of the court. A person who has a contempt filing against them is still entitled to a trial regarding whether they have violated the order or not.

Technically, for a court to find one has committed "contempt," the Judge must find the person knowingly disobeyed a "clear & unequivocal" order, and the violation "defeated, impaired, impeded or prejudiced" the rights of the other parent.

It should be noted that contempt of court is a potentially serious charge, and can have serious consequences if you are convicted. These consequences can include fines, having to pay for opposing counsel fees, changes in custody or visitation, and even jail time. If you are in this position, it would absolutely be in your best interest to seek legal representation before making your next move.

I've Been Accused of Violating a Custody Order. What Can I Do To Protect My Rights To Custody Of My Children?

If you have actually violated, or are violating, a custody order, the first thing you should do is to follow the order.

Some parents think they're entitled to withhold visitation if they feel the child's in danger (or doesn't want to go on the visit). Merely because there may be a basis to modify the prior order doesn't mean one is entitled to act as Judge, jury & executioner prior to a case being filed. If one thinks there's a basis to change a prior order, one should simply file a modification petition - and if there's an emergency, file an order to show cause along with an affidavit explaining what the emergency is[12].

---

[12] The form for an order to show cause may be found here: https://www.nycourts.gov/LegacyPDFS/FORMS/familycourt/pdfs/gf-1.pdf.

If you have any questions about whether you should follow certain provisions of the order, or you disagree with the allegation that you were violating the order in the first place, the best thing you can do is to consult an attorney on the issue right away. An attorney will be able to assess your side of the story and present it to the court in the most effective way possible.

I Have Primary Custody Of My Child. Do I Have The Right To Relocate With My Child If I Share Custody With Their Other Parent?

No, you do not have the right to relocate with you child if you share custody with the child's other parent[13]. Merely having primary custody of the child—or even having sole custody of the child—does not entitle you to relocate the residence of the child, at least not to a location far enough away that it would affect the non-custodial parent's visitation rights.

---

[13] See the Chapter below on "Relocating the Residence of Children."

This is a common misconception among parents who are awarded primary or sole custody of their children. They often believe having sole or primary residential custody allows them to move away without the court's permission. I often see parents who hold primary custody attempting to move 20, 40, even 50 miles away and farther, and expecting the court will not intervene. This is not the case.

Therefore, if you truly want or need to move to a location which is moderately far away from the child's other parent, you need (at the least) to obtain written, notarized permission from that non-custodial parent to do so. In addition, if you already have an order from either Divorce Court or Family Court addressing custody and visitation in your case, you should go back to court and get another order allowing the move as well. Even if the other side (i.e., the non-custodial parent) consents to your relocation, you should still go back to court and get an order that solidifies their consent. This way, no one can change their mind or wake up on the wrong side of the bed one morning and decide they don't consent to the move after all.

If the other parent doesn't consent to a move and you're already divorced, then you need to file an application with Family Court (or with Supreme Court). If you're still married, you need to file an application with Divorce Court - which is Supreme Court in New York.

* * *

Visitation Violations/Enforcement

If you are a non-custodial parent and you are not following the court ordered visitation schedule, the custodial parent can eventually go back to court and ask for visitation to be modified or scaled back. What happens next depends on why the non-custodial parent wasn't following through with the visitation schedule. If there is no valid reason for the non-custodial parent to keep missing visitation, then the visitation schedule is likely to be scaled back significantly.

However, if the non-custodial parent has a legitimate reason why they keep missing visits, such as a job, then the access schedule needs to be adjusted.

This often happens in cases where, during the initial proceedings, the lawyer for the non-custodial parent convinces them that they should ask for the most time possible - whether they can actually follow the resulting schedule or not. Then, when the parties get out of court, the non-custodial parent is consequently unable to follow through as a practical matter (e.g., due to work or other obligations). In these cases, the schedule can be easily modified by stipulation to accommodate both parents.

Can Custody Or Visitation In New York Ever Be Enforced Without Having A Final Court Order?

No - in New York, nothing of this nature is enforced without a court order. One may have a temporary court order pending more permanent court orders – interim orders *are* enforceable. However, if you have no court order whatsoever, then there is no way you can enforce custody or visitation.

This is the reason one should get some sort of a court order during the custody/visitation process. While some people only want a mere out-of-court "parenting agreement," it's best to incorporate the agreement into a court order. Otherwise, if it's violated by either parent, it can never be enforced. In fact, the only thing a person can do who has a co-parent violating a parenting agreement (without a court order) is file a petition to incorporate the agreement into a court order. Doing so still doesn't make previous violations of the agreement enforceable. Rather, it just makes it so that subsequent violations can be enforced.

Options Available To Have a Visitation Order Enforced In New York

The options depend on the order and the extent of the violations. However, one option in some cases is to go to the Supreme Court on an Order to Show Cause. Otherwise, enforcement of custody or visitation orders are usually done in Family Court. One would file either a Petition[14] (or if it's a more urgent issue, an

---

[14] The form for an Enforcement Petition may be found here: https://www.nycourts.gov/LegacyPDFS/FORMS/familycourt/pdfs/GF-41.pdf.

Order to Show Cause along with a Petition). If there is a deprivation of access, then one can also file a Writ of Habeas Corpus[15] - but this is almost always an application the custodial parent alone can file.

Should Someone Always Take The Matter To Court When One Party Violates A Custody Or Visitation Order?

This depends, once again, on the extent & context of the complaint. If the complaint is around a joint custody issue (a decision that needs to be made together on behalf of the child or the children) that you are just not able to agree on initially, it should not necessarily go straight to the court. There's often steps you can pursue to resolve these sorts of issues before going to court, such as consulting attorneys, consulting a friend, family member, or clergyman, sitting down

---

[15] The form for a Writ of Habeas Corpus may be found here: https://www.nycourts.gov/LegacyPDFS/FORMS/familycourt/pdfs/gf-23.pdf.

with specialists/experts/a social worker, and/or going into mediation[16].

You can also send a Default Notice Letter to the co-parent, bringing their attention to the fact that you believe they are violating the order and ask that they stop. In some cases, these letters can be effective, especially when they are sent by an attorney. They basically put the person on official notice that if the behavior does not stop, then you will make a contempt filing in court. It also helps in case you want to seek counsel fee awards for continued violations, because they won't be able to say they didn't know they were violating anything with their behavior.

---

[16] Especially if one already has a court order, one should go through the court for a referral to mediation. One does not necessarily need to have a pending case for such a referral. Information & key links to mediation may be found here: http://ww2.nycourts.gov/ip/adr/CourtPrograms.

There is no special format these letter must take – they can be as simple as an e-mail[17] providing a short summary of the alleged violation, reference to the portion of the order/agreement one feels is being violated, as well as a request to refrain from future violations and/or to contact the letter-writer to discuss remedies.

Will Police Ever Enforce A Custody Or Visitation Order In New York?

Generally – and in this context - the police only get involved if there is deprivation of access from a custodial parent. In the State of New York, a non-custodial parent withholding custody of a child from their custodial parent is called "custodial interference." It is a Class A misdemeanor within state lines. If the non-custodial parent brings the child

---

[17] Some agreements prescribe other methods and/or time-deadlines. Thus, one should consult one's settlement agreement or prior order.

across state lines, it is a felony. That's usually when the police will get involved.

Most other times, the police will only get involved if someone is alleging some kind of domestic violence, such as harassment or menacing or something along those lines. The police officer's primary job is to enforce criminal statutes. They are not really there to enforce Family Court orders. Oftentimes, if they are called out to the scene to enforce custody or visitation orders, they might informally talk to the parties and try calming them down. However, if there is still a dispute, they usually (merely) tell the people involved to bring the issue to the attention of a Family Court Judge.

Why Do I Need An Attorney To File A Motion To Enforce Child Visitation?

You don't necessarily *need* an attorney to file those sorts of Motions. There are forms online at nycourts.gov which can theoretically be used to draft one's own Petition[18]. In addition, when courts reopen after the COVID-19 shutdown, you can also physically go to the Court and have the clerks who work there assist you in drafting the various necessary Applications[19].

However, it is advisable to hire an attorney if you want the best chance at a good outcome for these Motions, Petitions, and Applications. Firstly, an attorney will make sure everything gets filed appropriately and on time, which often trips up self-filers. Perhaps more importantly, an attorney will know how to phrase the Petitions submitted to the Court so they will be compelling and considered valid by a Judge. You don't want to say too much or too little

---

[18] The link to the general page of the Court's custody & visitation forms may be found here: http://ww2.nycourts.gov/forms/familycourt/custodyvisitation.shtml.

[19] The courts generally have "Help Centers" to assist pro se litigants with drafting & filing petitions. The link for more information on them may be found here: https://www.nycourts.gov/CourtHelp/GoingToCourt/helpCenters.shtml.

in order to sustain your case, because in theory, a Judge could find you have insufficiently stated a basis for them to modify or enforce the Order, and then not even grant you a hearing or trial on it. If you want the best chance at a hearing, and success at that hearing, it behooves you to hire an attorney.

If A Motion To Enforce Visitation Is Granted, What Steps Will The Court In New York Take To Enforce It?

There are a number of things they can do, depending once again on the severity of the violation. They can switch custody of a child or children[20], increase or decrease visitation, make visitation supervised, or take visitation away altogether. They can also sanction a person in the form of either a monetary fine or an award of counsel fees. In theory, they can incarcerate someone or put them on

[20] In nearly all cases, the Judge will not switch custody of children without conducting a full "best interests" trial. At such a trial, the violation(s) of the visitation order will be considered as a factor (but 1 factor amongst many) in deciding whether to switch physical custody.

probation, but in my experience, this is very rarely done (in this context).

Conclusion

The bottom line is: it's always best to consult an attorney on these matters as early in the process as possible. You don't want to guess as to whether certain aspects are enforceable or modifiable, and you want a good attorney making your case. This means finding an attorney who specializes in family law. If you are considering hiring an attorney, ask them what percentage of their cases are divorce or family law cases. If they don't immediately answer that it's the majority of their practice (or better yet, the vast majority or the entirety of their practice), then they are really not a specialist. Attorneys who aren't specialists are more "jack of all trades" who accept anything that comes through their door. Generally you want to be wary of that. I always analogize in medical practice that if you have a really serious medical issue, you want to go to a specialist rather than a general practitioner. The same thing applies with law.

CHAPTER 4

RELOCATING THE RESIDENCE OF CHILDREN

There is no hard-and-fast exact rule on how far a custodial parent[21] can move with their child within New York State. However, generally

[21] In nearly all reported relocation cases, it's the custodial parent who is seeking to relocate the residence of the children. However, there are some cases in which a non-custodial parent seeks both physical custody and to relocate the residence of the children to another state.

speaking - and assuming the custodial parent does not have the other parent's permission or court permission - they would usually be allowed to move around 20-30 miles maximum[22] (without good justification for the move, that is). As aforementioned, there is no bright-line measure on how far a custodial parent would be allowed to move - unless the custody agreement or order entered into previously states a specific limit on distance.

Many (though not all) divorce settlement agreements that deal with child custody include a relocation clause. Relocation clauses put a specific geographical limit on how far away the custodial parent can move while retaining residential custody of the child. This limit is usually expressed as a space within a certain radius of their current residence. It serves as the "bright-line demarcation" that tells the

---

22 That said, I'm aware of 1 case which denied a move just 12-½ miles away from the current residence. *Schwartz v Schwartz*, 186 A.D.3d 1742, 132 N.Y.S.3d 34 (2d Dept 2020).

custodial parent exactly how far away they are permitted to move.

If there is no bright-line demarcation in a prior order or agreement and a custodial parent wants to move, analysis of the justification for the move is required. In particular, it must be ascertained whether the distance of the move would be so great as to impact the non-custodial parent's visitation rights, as well as their ability to participate in all other aspects of the child's life to the degree that they had been doing historically.

For example, let's say a non-custodial parent had been very involved with their child's extracurricular activities, including school events, plays, sporting events and things of that nature. If the non-custodial parent is very involved in these activities, then the custodial parent moving even 20 miles away (especially if living in an urban area with long commute times) could be considered an undue infringement on the non-custodial parent's rights. This is because it adds an additional 20 miles of travel each way for the non-custodial parent, which they have to undergo every time they want to participate in their child's life (as they had been doing historically up until that point).

Sometimes it's not just the mileage. For instance, in New York City, 20 miles could be a tremendous amount of time to travel, so the court would also take that into consideration as well. I have seen moves as short as 12 miles away be disapproved by the courts. Some Judges are considering that "it's not just the mileage that matters, it's also the time that it's going to take" - especially if the non-custodial parent already had joint custody and was very involved in every aspect of the child's life.

What Factors Will The Court Consider When Determining Whether A Parent Can Relocate With The Child?

In New York State, we have a leading decision on relocation called *Tropea*[23]. In a nutshell, *Tropea*

---

[23] https://www.nycourts.gov/reporter/archives/tropea.htm.

basically says that the court should consider all circumstances surrounding the reasons or justifications for a potential move. Generally speaking, moving a child is disfavored to the extent it will impact or impede the non-custodial parent's visitation rights. Some examples of specific factors the court takes into consideration when considering a move include:

- Each parent's reasons for seeking or opposing the move
- The quality of the relationship between the child and both the custodial parent
- The quality of the relationship between the child and the non-custodial parent
- The specific impact of the move on both the quantity and quality of the child's future contact with the non-custodial parent
- The degree to which the custodial parent and the child's life may be enhanced economically, emotionally and/or educationally by the move
- The feasibility of preserving the relationship between the child and the non-custodial parent

through suitable visitation arrangements if the move is approved.

- The involvement of the non-custodial parent in the child's life and with the child historically up to the point of relocation. That is, how often the parent actually visits the child, and how involved the parent is in various areas of the child's everyday life (i.e., schooling, extracurricular activities, sports, playdates, vacations, etc.).
- The child's preferences (to the degree that the child is old and mature enough to appreciate the potential impact of a relocation on their relationship with the non-custodial parent).

This is not an exhaustive list, but it hits the main factors which are usually considered when a court decides whether to allow a custodial parent to move with a child.

See **Appendix B** for a sample chart, which should assist you with organizing your evidence & witnesses for trial.

Can I Move Out Of State With My Child?

Moving out of state with a child is more of a classic relocation situation. Generally speaking, you will need either notarized, written consent from the non-custodial parent (at the least), and/or court permission. Again, as aforementioned, the analysis really is how involved that non-custodial parent has been with the child and all aspects of the child's life, as well as what reasons the custodial parent has to justify the move.

It should be noted that in these cases, the court prioritizes what it believes to be in the best interest *of the child*. Though the best interests of each parent are represented, they are not the prime concern of the court.

Potential reasons for wanting to relocate to a different state are judged on the metric of how the move might benefit versus how much the move might harm the development of the child - as well as the child's relationship with the nonmoving parent. Reasons that seem overly concerned with the interests of the parents (especially when they do not seem to coincide provably or directly with the interests of the child) are more likely to be disapproved by the courts.

For instance, if the custodial parent comes to the court and says they want to move to Connecticut simply because "Connecticut is a nicer state", or they want a "fresh start", it is unlikely their reasoning will be considered sufficient justification to allow a move out of state, especially if it stands to impede the rights of the other parent.

But again, everything in these matters is fact-specific, and there are some instances where the facts of the case might support that same justification. Let's say, for instance, the non-custodial parent in the Connecticut case has been largely uninvolved with the child. In that case, the court is much more likely to approve relocation to another state, even in cases where the justification for moving isn't all that strong.

Another leading reasons for approving - or denying - a relocation is the ability to maintain a relationship between the children & the nonmoving parent. As such, there is really a balancing of the various factors in determining whether to approve an out-of-state move.

Can I Ever Move Out Of New York State With My Child Without The Other Parent's Permission?

Yes, in some cases you may move out of New York State with your child without the non-custodial parent's permission. However, in order to do so, you must obtain the permission of the court. If you don't have 1 of those 2, then you risk a Judge ordering you to return the child to New York at your expense - and may even risk losing custody.

The way you get the court's permission in this sort of case depends on whether you are already divorced. If you are already divorced, then you have a divorce judgment in place. This judgment may already have a relocation clause. Regardless, in order to apply to the court for permission to move out of New York State as an already divorced person, one option is to file an Order to Show Cause in the Supreme Court. This Order to Show Cause will seek the Judge's permission to relocate. If you were never married, you can file a Custody Petition in Family Court, specifically seeking relocation.

Filing these documents will usually trigger a relocation trial, which may take some time. In some extreme emergencies, the courts will expedite the trial. In general, the courts do try to expedite relocation cases more quickly than a "normal custody determination" - but even so, they oftentimes take many months to get a resolution from a Judge. It can take even longer if there were no prior custody determinations in the first place. If you are coming to court for the very first time to seek relocation and you don't even have a custody order in place, then the process may take as long as a year or more.

It should be noted that each court varies in its wait times, and circumstances vary within each individual court. As this book is being finalized, in December, 2021, we're still going through a pandemic and the effects of COVID-19 on local, state, and federal courts. Many courts are taking even longer than usual to make determinations because of tremendous backlogs. In general, I would advise potential applicants to be prepared for a long process/long wait times before receiving approval for relocation.

My Child's Custodial Parent Wants to Move Away with Our Child. Is There Anything I Can Do To Stop That?

Yes, if your child's custodial parent wants to move away with your child, there are certain things you can do to try to stop that.

The first thing you should do is to immediately write a formal letter to the custodial parent, making it crystal clear you object to the move. For example, I had a client who expressed dismay at the impending move, but a review of the texts/e-mails did not reveal his clear objection to the move. This was later exploited by the mother's attorney at trial.

You can also head-off the process. If they let you know either orally or in writing, "Hey, I'm moving in a week," or "I'm moving in two weeks," you can go into the Supreme Court or Family Court and file an Order to Show Cause – a type of emergency motion. Your Order to Show Cause will ask the Judge to issue an Interim Order restricting the custodial parent from relocating the residence of the child until the Judge can decide on whether to approve the move. Timing is of the essence in these matters, and you should act on this as soon as you possibly can.

I have represented clients on both sides of the fence in relocation cases. I have often seen cases where the custodial parent has said, "I plan on moving," and the non-custodial parent really didn't do much of anything about it. In their inaction, they allowed the custodial parent to move, and then they decide they don't like the result and go into court after the move. At that point, sometimes the Judge will order the custodial parent to move back, and sometimes they won't. Sometimes they will allow the custodial parent and the child to remain in their new location pending a full trial. And if the child(ren) have been residing in the new state for many months before the trial is conducted, bank on the fact that the custodial parent will argue at trial that the Judge shouldn't order them to return because "they've come accustomed to their new environment."

What to Do If My Petition to Relocate With My Child Is Denied?

If you are a custodial parent and a Judge denies your relocation petition after a hearing or trial, there are steps you can take. After the Judge issues their decision, you will get a final Order to that effect. You have a right to appeal that Order, keeping in mind you generally only have 30 days to file the Notice of your intention to appeal (called a "Notice of Appeal"). Generally, if you miss the deadline, then you're not going to be able to appeal to the next highest court. There are exceptions to this rule – e.g., sometimes they make exceptions if there has been no "Notice of Entry" of the final order that got served on you. Nevertheless, you should really act immediately to challenge the Order.

Now, ultimately if the Judge says, "You can't move" and you either don't appeal or you do appeal and you lose the appeal that means that you can't move[24]. If you do move and you violate a Judge's

---

[24] Though one in theory has the ability to appeal to the NY Court of Appeal – the highest court in the state. However, the Court of

order, in all likelihood the Judge is going to strongly consider taking the child away from you and putting the child in the custody of the other parent. It would be a bad move on one's part to disregard a Judge's order.

That said, if the custodial parent is seeking relocation, they should also strongly consider filing for child support. If they already have a support order in place, filing an upward modification of the support order will fulfil the same purpose. This is a way to "cover your bases," so to speak, as marked steps you have taken to try to get more financial support before opting to move.

To illustrate this point, let's say there's a custodial parent who wants to move from the NYC area to Pennsylvania with their child. Let's say one of the stated reasons the parent is seeking to relocate is financial (i.e., they say they want to move to Pennsylvania because the greater NYC area is becoming too expensive). This issue will come up at

---

Appeals only accepts about 10% of requests to appeal to that court - and far less than half of those cases are reversed.

trial. Opposing counsel may ask you if you sought increased child support if you were struggling with meeting NYC costs. If you have done so, that is one less roadblock they can put in the way of your move.

Requesting child support or increased child support payments also has another upside when it comes to relocation. The custodial parent may consider that child support can function as a sort of bargaining chip over the non-custodial parent. For instance, you can say to the non-custodial parent, "I'll cut you a deal on child support if you're willing to agree on the relocation." Indeed, it's a specific statutory factor on child support if the non-custodial parent incurs "extraordinary visitation expenses" in order to exercise their visitation.

As such, child support can be considered both a factor and a negotiation tool. Ultimately, if the non-custodial parent is going to object to the relocation, the custodial parent can use that financial leverage to try to get the non-custodial parent to the bargaining table. At the very least, asking for child support or a child support increase will put more money in your pocket, which may help you deal with the higher costs of staying in a more expensive area (if a financially based move is not approved).

CHAPTER 5

ALIMONY MODIFICATION & ENFORCEMENT

There are several reasons to request alimony (maintenance) modification.

The most common requests are for "downward modification" (lowering the payments), coming from the person paying alimony (the "alimony payor.") They are usually connected with some type of unemployment or underemployment. In this sense, the common reasons given for alimony modification requests are similar those given for requests for child support modification.

Alimony payors also commonly request downward modification if the alimony recipient remarries. In that case, there is an almost an automatic basis for modification or even termination of alimony maintenance.

On the flipside, it is also possible for alimony recipients to request "upward modification" (increasing the payments). This usually happens if there was either a provision in the party settlement agreement allowing for upward modification, or if there was a similar decision after trial. In any case, upward modification requests are almost always made because, due to a substantial change of circumstances, the payments are no longer sufficient to meet the alimony recipient's needs.

In these cases, the court usually applies a standard referred to as "undue financial hardship to the party" in order to decide whether a request for upward modification should be granted. In order to meet that standard, it needs to be established that the recipient is incapable of supporting him/herself.

When Can An Alimony Agreement Be Modified In New York?

Usually, an alimony (maintenance) *agreement*[25] can only be modified under the standard of unforeseen or unanticipated change of circumstances. This is why parties need to be very careful in crafting their settlement agreements. If they even remotely anticipate that circumstances may change within the duration of maintenance, they need to add specific provisions for those changes if they want to be able to adjust their agreement accordingly.

Duration is an important term in this context. Alimony maintenance can theoretically be a permanent award that goes on until one party is deceased. However, in nearly every case, it is set or fixed by duration: that is, maintenance ends after a fixed amount

---

[25] This would almost always be a section within one's divorce settlement agreement.

of time, be it 2 years or 5 years or 10 years. If there is a change of circumstances within that period of time, your settlement agreement must specifically allow for modification in order for the payments to be adjusted. If your agreement does not stipulate that it can be modified, then you are essentially locked into the payments the agreement lays out.

This may serve neither the payor nor the recipient. On the payor's end, it locks you into set payments whether or not you can continue to afford them, given your change of circumstances. On the recipient's end, it locks you into set payments whether or not they are sufficient, given your change of circumstances.

How Soon After A Divorce Is Final Could Someone Apply For A Modification to Alimony?

In theory, somebody could apply for a modification to alimony (Maintenance) right away. However, it would not generally make sense to do so. The issue when it comes to alimony modification is not necessarily how much time has passed, but rather *what* (in terms of financial circumstances) has changed. To measure what has changed, the court looks at what has occurred between the date of the application for modification and the date that the alimony agreement was filed and entered into an agreement of divorce. If they are very close together, the chances of proving a change in circumstances are quite slim.

In some cases, however, it makes sense to file for a modification to alimony relatively soon after an alimony settlement is filed. Let's say the settlement was entered into in January of 2021. If in April of 2021, the payor loses his or her job unexpectedly, that could serve as a basis to apply for downward modification on alimony or maintenance. In this example, even though the time period in question is quite short, it represents an arguably significant change in circumstances.

Factors the Court Considers When Dealing With a Modification of Alimony Petition

There are a number of things the court considers when looking at a modification of alimony (maintenance) petition.

One of the first considerations is whether the filer crosses the initial threshold of proving a substantial, unanticipated change of circumstances (when the maintenance was established in a divorce settlement agreement). If the alimony agreement allows for modification and the filer can prove certain basic elements of the unanticipated change of circumstance, then it essentially reopens the maintenance issue.

At that point, the court considers the same factors that they consider in any maintenance award. The primary considerations are the respective incomes of the parties, the assets & property of each party, the ability to pay along with the reason the payor lost his/her job (on a downward modification case). On the latter factor, if the Judge feels the loss of job or income was self-induced, the modification may be denied. On the recipient's end, the court examines their ability to be self-supporting, whether they have a job, and what their expenses are, as compared to what the payor's expenses are.

Once the threshold of evidence for a change of circumstance is passed, all of the above factors would be potentially admissible at a hearing or trial on the issue of modification of maintenance.

If There Is No Evidence Regarding A Significant Change In Circumstances, Will The Petition To Modify Alimony Be Dismissed By The Court?

If you present no evidence regarding a significant change in circumstances, your petition can—and should—be dismissed. If one files a motion, one should support it with the relevant documentary evidence that would corroborate the testimony given in one's affidavit.

For instance, if a payor has been laid off, they should include evidence supporting that fact. This could be a letter from their former employer directly confirming they have been laid off, or a receipt for unemployment payments, which would be indirect evidence they've lost their job through no fault of their own.

If it's the recipient who is filing and alleging a change of circumstances, they should also corroborate their affidavit with documentation to show why or how their circumstances have changed. For instance, if they just got evicted from their apartment or lost their lease, then they can include a letter from their former landlord or documents from Housing Court. If they lost a 2d job (which they had at the time of the original divorce, but didn't provide enough income to meet their needs), they should provide the same corroborating evidence the payor would provide if they lost their job.

Ultimately, though, your case is built on evidence. You need to be able to show what you are claiming. If your case goes before the court, the judge will examine it closely. If they ask what evidence you have to corroborate your claim, and you say you don't have any, then the court should—and almost certainly will—dismiss your application.

Hearing Schedule after Filing the Petition for Modification of Alimony

It usually takes several months or more for a hearing to be scheduled once a Petition for Modification of Alimony is filed.

The actual time frame depends largely on where you file the application. When it comes to alimony modification, filing in Family Court tends to be somewhat faster than filing in Supreme Court. If speed is your priority, it's recommended you file in Family Court. Still, even considering the relative speediness of Family Court, you may be looking at a process lasting approximately 6 months. If you file in Supreme Court, the process usually takes 6-12 months.

If There Is An Emergency Financial Hardship, Will The New York Courts Hear The Order Sooner?

Yes – in such instance, one should file an Order to Show Cause, which is often filed in emergencies, and wedge in the application. In an Order to Show Cause, you can state in bold print—right in the first couple of paragraphs of the affidavit—that there is an emergency, with all of the important details. This will have the effect of bringing the change of circumstances into focus for the Judge, as well as the urgent need for adjustments to accommodate for the change.

If you have an attorney filing on your behalf, they can even include a cover letter alerting the court to the emergency and requesting the soonest available court date.

What Is The Impact Of Cohabitation On Alimony In New York?

In the State of New York, if the agreement does not say otherwise, then mere cohabitation between the recipient or the payor and a third-party does nothing to alimony or maintenance. By statute, it is only if the recipient is holding him or herself out as married to a third-party that may create a basis to modify maintenance or alimony.

However, sometimes agreements will provide otherwise. Individual agreements can deviate from the statute and provide conditions that are binding within the agreement. For instance, an agreement can state that if a recipient chooses to cohabitate with someone of the opposite sex for more than 3 or 4 months, it can create a basis to modify maintenance.

I often find such provisions to be problematic, and sometimes frankly homophobic in the way that they exclude the possibility of same-sex relationships. Generally, one should be wary about writing provisions like this into agreements. Merely having a boyfriend or girlfriend or significant other should not really do anything to a person's maintenance or alimony - the same as choosing to have a roommate should not necessarily do anything to a person's maintenance or alimony. The mere fact that the recipient has engaged in a romantic relationship also shouldn't change the analysis on what they are entitled to in terms of alimony or maintenance, and according to statute, it doesn't. If one wishes to argue that cohabitation with another may help defray living expenses of the recipient – and thus s/he doesn't need as much maintenance at that point – then a mere "substantial change of circumstances" provision in the agreement should allow the Court to consider modification in that instance. However, if both parties entered into an agreement that provides for modification under specific circumstances (including cohabitation), then those are the terms of the agreement.

Are There Any Situations That Would Result In Automatic Termination Of Alimony?

Yes - by statute, two events can automatically terminate alimony or maintenance: the remarriage of the recipient, and the death of either party. However, while these events are grounds for termination of alimony or maintenance, the court will not know that they occurred unless someone files an application saying so. Your application will almost always be accepted in those instances, but you are required to actually file the application in order to have the termination made official by the court.

If An Order To Modify Alimony Is Granted, Can It Ever Be Reverted Once Circumstances Normalize?

The answer to this question is yes, in theory.

If a modification order is granted in either direction (either up or down), you can request that the Judge require each party is to turn over their finances on at least an annual basis, so that either party can assess whether circumstances have changed and require another modification application.

As an example, let's say the payor loses his or her job and is granted a downward modification of maintenance based on the loss of income. In that case, the recipient should ask the Judge for one of two things.

The first possibility is requesting a two-step order. This means that the court will grant the payor reduced alimony or maintenance payments for a certain amount of time (say, the next 6 months or the next 12 months). However, when that time is up, the payor is required to apply for further modification. If they do not, or if they reapply and their application is denied, then the original agreement will automatically be reinstated.

The second possibility is requesting a provision in the modification order saying that the payor needs to turn over their finances on at least an annual basis, or to affirmatively notify the recipient if they get a job. So, under those circumstances, if they lose their job and then get a great paying job and can then afford to pay the original amount of maintenance, the recipient can file an application with the court and ask for a reinstatement of the original amount.

Nevertheless, as stated above, most divorces are resolved by divorce settlement agreement. In such instance, courts encourage finality to agreements and discourage parties coming back to court every few years to modify agreements. Unless the standard has been changed (from "unanticipated change of circumstances"), then it remains quite hard to change the maintenance amount or duration. And if the payor fails in his/her application for a downward modification application, chances are the recipient will ask the court to award her/him reimbursement for the counsel fees spent in defending the action.

* * *

Enforcement of Spousal Support Orders

The (recommended) first step is to issue a default notice letter, highlighting the time lapsed since the last payment was due. The letter should request information regarding the reason for missed payment and ask that the payment be made - as well as requiring a response within ten days of the of the date of the letter or email. Perhaps the other side has some valid reason to explain the missed payments, or the parties can otherwise negotiate a payment schedule to get back on track. In these cases, a stipulation can be drawn up by an attorney and court may be avoided.

If no adequate response is received, then there is the option to remedy the situation in court.

What Options Are Available To Enforce A Spousal Support Order In New York?

After filing a default notice letter, if no appropriate response has been received, a petition should be filed in Supreme Court, or Family Court, requesting that the former spouse be held in violation of the court order. In Family Court, the form is the same as that used for enforcement of child support orders (and thus can be amended to specify its enforcement of a spousal support order). The form is here: https://www.nycourts.gov/LegacyPDFS/FORMS/familycourt/pdfs/4-13.pdf.

If the court finds the payor of alimony willfully violated the order and has no reasonable excuse to have missed payment, then counsel fee reimbursement is mandatory. Some may be reluctant to go back to court because it involves hiring an attorney - but it is important to note the party not following the support order will generally be compelled to pay the incurred legal fees of the recipient.

How to Prove That the Alimony Order Is Not Being Followed By My Former Spouse?

Typically, all that is required is an affidavit stating the terms of the order, declaring the payments that have been received and the payments that have not been received. Bank account statements may be used as supporting evidence if direct payments should be received, however this level of support is not always necessary as proof with an initial application. Once an allegation that an order has not been followed, the burden shifts to the other side to prove either they have made the payments or they have a valid defense as to why they are not obligated (or able) to make the payments.

Can I Always Take My Ex-Spouse To Court If They Violate A Spousal Support Order?

No - court is not always the answer. Again, it is recommended to first send off a default notice letter bringing formal attention to the other side that you are alleging they are violating the order and give them a period of time (usually within ten days) to make payment. Some agreements do provide for as long as 20-30 days, so it is important to consult one's divorce settlement agreement to see what period is specified. A default notice is not required - unless your agreement says otherwise - but it is advisable to do so, unless there is reason to believe the other side is intentionally ignoring the order. If the other party has a reasonable defense, such as being unaware that an employer was not sending payment, it is likely the issue can be rectified without a formal court hearing.

I'm Being Held In Contempt For Failing To Comply With My Spousal Support Order, What Does This Mean?

Contempt of court means the other side is alleging one intentionally violated the court's order. If you are found to have willfully violated the order for alimony or spousal support, the top penalty for this violation (although rarely imposed) is jail time. If there is no track record of one violating the court order, then the court can impose a money judgment. They can authorize the other side to garnish wages, seize bank account assets or retirement/investment assets. In some cases, the court can authorize the person to seize property to satisfy any arrears. If served with a contempt application, one should consult with an attorney immediately to discuss options for a valid defense to that application[26].

Do I Need An Attorney To Enforce An Alimony Or Spousal Support Order?

Not necessarily, but it is always advisable to (at least) consult with an attorney. One can file one's own petition - the court forms are found at www.nycourts.gov/forms/index.shtml.

---

[26] One should note many of the recommendations in the chapter below on child support enforcement are also applicable to defending oneself in a spousal support enforcement case.

There are forms readily adaptable for orders to show cause, as well as petitions in family court. An individual can download these, complete the forms, and submit them to the court. However, it is wise to take thirty to sixty minutes to consult with an attorney for assurance the forms are completed correctly before submitting to the court. Many attorneys offer low-cost consultations. Although these forms can be filed by the individual, it is prudent to have an attorney represent them at all stages of legal proceedings, particularly where one is trying to enforce an order of the court.

Can Spousal Support Be Garnished From Wages In New York?

If a fixed dollar amount and timing of payment is captured within the judgment, an income deduction order can be issued by the court. The form to initiate an income deduction order can be found here: https://www.nycourts.gov/LegacyPDFS/FORMS/familycourt/pdfs/4-9a-LDSS-5038.pdf. Moreover, instructions for the form may be found here: https://www.nycourts.gov/LegacyPDFS/FORMS/familycourt/pdfs/4-9b-LDSS-5039.pdf.

For example, if the court orders the payment of $1,000 a month be paid on the first of each month, it is easy to draw up an income execution which must be implemented by a court or attorney. It is possible to seek to register the spousal support order with collection units, specifying a dollar amount that is payable at fixed periods of time, though the Support Collection Unit usually will only enforce spousal support if it's in conjunction with a child support order.

What Happens If I Can No Longer Afford To Pay Alimony?

In New York State, one would need to demonstrate a substantial change in circumstances since the initial order or judgment of divorce, to effect change in the order[27]. An individual would need to prove why their circumstances changed and that the change is no fault of their own; for instance, one was laid off and the job shipped overseas. In this example, it would be the responsibility of the paying party to demonstrate the

---

[27] See the section above on modification of maintenance.

change in employment and submit a diligent job search to prove to the court they have an inability to find work that is commensurate with their prior earnings.

The burden of proof is on the payor and modification is not generally granted upon their own say so. Very rarely will an order be outright terminated due to an inability to pay. Usually if one side files an enforcement application, and the defense is an inability to pay, then a cross motion or a counter petition asking for modification will be filed. The issues would then be intertwined, and the court would either find that they intentionally violated the order or that they are entitled to a temporary downward modification of the spousal support order.

Thus, if the recipient of maintenance files a violation petition in court - and the payor can't afford the payments, the payor should file a modification petition - and may even consider filing a petition for relief of the maintenance arrears. The form for the latter application may be found here: https://www.nycourts.gov/LegacyPDFS/FORMS/familycourt/pdfs/4-15.pdf.

CHAPTER 6

ENFORCEMENT REGARDING THE DIVISION OF ASSETS

The court can enforce the division of property and assets within a divorce decree in New York. If there is a settlement agreement (which is the case in about 95-98% of divorces), then the parties would just follow the settlement agreement and judgment of divorce. If the settlement agreement requires them to sell a house, they would just sell the house on their own.

There is no real mechanism to police that except in the violation. If, in this example, the settlement agreement says you have to sell a house within a certain period of time and one party refuses, the remedy is to file an application with the court to enforce the divorce decree. Then the court can decide to do many things - as examples, they can grant counsel fees in the violation, they can sanction a person for violating the order, and they can issue a specific order taking away the ability of the party to jointly consent to brokers or set listing prices.

If there are continued violations, the court can eventually appoint one party or the other to be the "receiver" to sell the property. In other words, they will not need the other party's signature or consent to sell the property.

Are Child Support or Spousal Maintenance Ever Part of the Property Division in A Divorce Decree?

Yes, child support or spousal maintenance absolutely can be a part of the property division in a divorce decree. Those issues can be components of a property division resolution. Both maintenance and support are also factors the court would take into consideration in property division and asset division. Usually, however, the agreements are global settlements. In other words, as part of the division of property and assets, there will also be in a separate section of the settlement agreement regarding maintenance and child support. But it's all part of one package. A common way to settle maintenance and/or child support is to give a party more or less of the property and assets. Likewise, you can give a party more maintenance and less support or vice versa.

All of these three issues - the asset/property division, the maintenance, and the child support - can all play off each other to structure which one would be best for both parties. Parties are recommended to consult either a certified financial planner or an accountant for extra advice on which would make the best financial sense for them, especially if they are looking to play one off against the other.

What If My Ex-Spouse Does Not Do What The Judge Orders In The Property Division?

Most agreements require the parties to send out a "default notice letter." More recently, that is usually done just by email, but it can be by certified mail - but double-check your agreement to see if it specifies a particular method.

This letter is basically just calling the violator's attention to the fact they are violating the agreement and they have a certain number of days, usually 30 days. Some agreements say 10 or 20 days to rectify the alleged violation. In other words, you are specifically saying: "you are violating the agreement," refer to the section in the agreement and say "this is why I think you are violating the agreement and if you disagree, please let me know why you think that you are not violating the agreement" and why you think you are in compliance.

If the other side does not respond or, more importantly, doesn't rectify the violation, then the other party alleging the violation can file an application in the court. It is common s/he will attach to their application a copy of the default notice letter saying they tried to avoid court. This in effect says to the Court "I sent this letter out to this other party, they ignored it (or at least didn't rectify the violation) and that's why I am here." Doing so sets themselves up *even better* for an award of counsel fees or sanctions, which they should request in New York.

How Long Do I Have To Request Enforcement Of A Division Of Property Order In New York?

There is no specific timeframe unless your agreement says otherwise. At the same time, you do not want to let it go many years because at some point, the other side will have a defense called "latches" - which means, in a nutshell, if you sit on your rights at some point you lose them.

So, if there is an alleged violation one should file your enforcement action at least within either several months or not more than about a year or so after the violation because again, at some point, it becomes stale. Indeed, the longer one waits to file an enforcement application, the more likely it'll be that the Judge will do little more than give a "warning" that both sides must follow the agreement/order.

What Can't A New York Enforcement Order Do When It Comes To Property And Assets?

There are many things an order cannot do when it comes to property and assets. An order of enforcement cannot require a party to jump backwards through a flaming hoop is one example. There is also "public policy" which means that orders cannot violate provisions of common decency, but also where the courts or the legislature has determined that something is not proper to be inserted into those types of orders.

For example, an order cannot generally erase child support arrears. Even if somebody has been found to violate a property division or asset division issue, the court cannot punish this person by vacating child support s/he would otherwise be entitled to, because that would be against public policy.

Likewise, orders cannot bar a party from seeking child support in the future - as a penalty for violating other aspects of the agreement.

Moreover, while jail is theoretically a possible penalty for contempt of court, it's very rare for a court to order a person jailed for violating the property/asset aspects of a divorce settlement agreement.

When Can I File A Motion To Enforce The Division Of Property In New York?

You are able to file a motion to enforce the division of property in New York at any time. Usually, your agreement requires you to send out the "default notice letter" first. You should do that first before you file your application, and then wait for the number of days specified in your agreement to see if you get a response or if the other party rectifies the violation. After that time period is over, go ahead and file. There is no timeframe beyond that which you have to wait.

As such, if you've already tried to resolve the conflict with a default notice letter, then your next step is to file an order to show cause to enforce the property or asset distribution. The general form for the order to show cause may be found here: https://www.nycourts.gov/LegacyPDFS/forms/matrimonial/PS-Contempt-OSC.pdf. The motion must be accompanied by an affidavit in support - the form of which may be found here: https://www.nycourts.gov/LegacyPDFS/forms/matrimonial/PS-ContemptOrder-Affidavit.pdf. You should also attach as "exhibits" to the motion any documents which corroborate your claim - such as the judgment of divorce, the settlement agreement and the default notice letter (among others).

Then the court can do many things. The court may need to hold a factual hearing to determine whether the person had a valid reason for refusing to comply with either the buyout or the sale of the property or the signature of the deed. But if the person does not have a valid defense, then the court can order the property to be sold without their consent or dispense with their need to sign off on any of the papers by appointing a receiver.

What If It Is Unclear How The Property Was Divided In A New York Divorce?

If it is unclear how the property was divided in a New York divorce, the court would review the agreement in an effort to ascertain the parties' intentions. Otherwise, the court may need to have a hearing on the issue to decide what should be done. Both parties will have to present testimony and evidence as to how they want the property divided as well as the intent of particular clauses of their agreement.

What If My Ex-Spouse Does Not Comply With The Order For Delivery Of Property Or Assets?

If you've already been to court for the violation once - and the party still does not follow the court's order, then you should follow the same game plan as stated above.

As such, send them a "default notice letter" by email or certified mail (the method depending on the wording of the agreement). If the violation is not remedied, one must then file another order to show cause for enforcement with the court.

The court will determine whether the other party had a valid reason for holding up the sale or transfer of assets. If they do, the court may need to have a hearing on the issue. The other party could be found in violation. In this case, the court can do one of many things: sanction them, award counsel fees, or take away their power to consent to a broker. If the issue is the other party refusing to sign over the deed, the Judge can enter an order putting the other person in charge of the property as "receiver" of the property.

Who Pays The Cost For The Proceeding To Enforce The Division Of Property Or Assets In A Divorce Decree In New York?

Initially the person bringing the application, if they hire an attorney, will have to pay their attorney money to go into court. They will also have to pay the motion fee for filing an order to show cause in New York (as of this writing, the fee is $45 to file a motion)[28]. They will need to pay the process server to serve the

[28] https://nycourts.gov/forms/filingfees.shtml.

other side. But if the court finds that the violator willfully violated the divorce settlement agreement and a judgment of divorce, the court has the power to direct them to reimburse - not only counsel fees - but also the cost of bringing the proceeding, as well as process service costs.

When Should I Talk To A Lawyer About Enforcing A Property Division Order In My Divorce Settlement?

You should talk to a lawyer even before you serve the default notice letter – especially if you are not sure exactly how to phrase it. If you are sure you're following the divorce settlement agreement as to the method & timing, then you can go ahead and do it on your own. Then, if the person does not comply with the settlement after you serve the default notice letter that is the point in time when you should definitely consult an attorney, so that you know exactly how to proceed and the exact format of the papers that you have to file.

CHAPTER 7

MODIFICATION & ENFORCEMENT OF CHILD SUPPORT ORDERS

What Exactly Is a Downward Modification of Support?

A downward modification of support is a request that the amount of child support is reduced in some way as a result of various factors. This can happen if one parent's income has gone up or down, or if the original support order changes due to the circumstances within the family. For instance, if there were three children on the support order, and one of them was emancipated, the order would need to be recalculated based on the new set of conditions.

Another common reason for a downward modification of support is if one parent or the other loses their job. Usually, in this case, the non-custodial parent would lose their job and would want support adjusted accordingly.

What Are Legitimate Reasons for The Inability To Pay Support At The Current Level Ordered By The Courts In New York?

This depends on whether somebody had a divorce settlement agreement or not. If the couple had a divorce settlement agreement done, then the attorney would need to determine when the settlement was executed, and what was agreed upon for child support. In 2010, New York state law modified the law such that any agreements executed after 2010[29] are now subject to the statutory modification standards (see below). However, agreements done before 2010[30] remain bound to the previous legislation known as "unanticipated change of circumstances." This requires that something unforeseen must have happened that caused the person to have a reduction of income.

Although many people claim they lost their job due to unanticipated circumstances, there must be facts which support the claim. This can include an extended duration of employment and stability of the job itself. However, if the person had frequent career changes and was in a relatively new position at the time of the agreement, then it's harden to prove the loss of job was "unanticipated." Above all, an attorney (and ultimately the Judge) must determine what the divorce settlement agreement was and what was settled on regarding the ability to modify support.

---

[29] More precisely, the effective date of the change is October 13, 2010.

[30] The agreements may also "opt-out" of the modification standards or otherwise change the standards.

As of 2010, child support can be modified under one of the three circumstances:

- There has been a "substantial change of circumstances."
- There has been a 15% difference in income since the support order was last set or adjusted.
- Three years has passed since the original order was set or last modified.

This is now the statutory basis to modify support in New York - unless the parties have executed a divorce settlement agreement "opting out" of the statutory basis to modify. If an individual satisfies one of these three requirements to change support, it does not necessarily mean the Judge will ultimately change the support order. Once the parent satisfies one of these three grounds to modify support, their support case is reopened, and the court must calculate a new support order based on the statutory and case-law standards.

If you lost your job, you must also prove that (a) you lost the job thru no fault of your own (i.e., you were not fired due to misconduct, nor did you voluntarily quit) and (b) you made a diligent search to find new work commensurate with your prior earnings, work history, education & skills. One is well-recommended to keep a "job search diary" to help document all efforts to find new work. One should make looking for work a full-time job in itself – i.e., let the Judge see you've spent an average of 30-40 hours weekly looking for work.

The "job search diary" is best kept on a computer – but one may also keep a hard-copy of it in a 3-ring binder. One should generally document at least 30-40 "job efforts" per week. "Job efforts" may consist of numerous tasks – applying for work, going to job fairs, going to the Dept. of Labor, studying for & taking civil service exams (local, state & federal), taking courses in resume & interviewing skills, etc. You should record and document (with print-outs and copies) all job applications, internet submissions, phone calls, in-person inquiries, etc. and the results thereof for each job you apply to or inquire about.

If you are medically unable to work, you will need a letter from your doctor stating his/her diagnosis, the date(s) of treatment, and his/her prognosis, including any limitations on work you may have, when you may be expected to go back to work, whether & when you may be able to perform office work and/or light duties or part-time work. The letter should contain an affirmation of your Doctor stating "s/he is authorized by law to practice in New York, s/he is not a party to this action, and s/he affirms the contents of this report to be true under penalties of perjury." While I can, upon your request, assist you in getting the proper letter from your doctor, you should understand that ultimately this is your responsibility to get this letter from the doctor in time for the court date. Indeed, it is my advice that you get me this letter well in advance of the Court date. **You should also immediately submit an application for disability** to the extent you have not done so already (https://www.ssa.gov/disabilityssi/).

If you perform any odd jobs (i.e., jobs for which you will not receive a W-2 at the end of the year for), then you must keep an "Odd Jobs diary," which lists - for each day you perform such work - who you worked for, the type of work you performed each day, the rate of pay and how much you received (broken down by pay received each day and/or total for the job if it lasts multiple days).

The format for a "Job Search Diary" can be found in **Appendix C**.

How Do I Apply for A Downward Modification of Support in New York Family Court?

Post-pandemic, the court system has allowed e-filing of support petitions. You can obtain a modification petition via the court's website: http://ww2.nycourts.gov/forms/familycourt/childsupport.shtml.

Once you complete it, then you can just e-file it through the court's EDDS system (link here: https://iappscontent.courts.state.ny.us/NYSCEF/live/edds.htm), which is the electronic delivery system where people can self-file petitions as opposed to paper filings done at the courthouse. Once somebody files the petition, they should hear back from the court within a week or two after filing with their court dates. The court will then send them a summons, and they can go ahead and start preparing the initial paperwork for the hearing, which will be set about two months after they file.

An alternative way a person can file a downward modification petition is to file an order to show cause in the Supreme Court. Although this is an option, it is generally better to file a downward modification petition in Family Court (if that is the only issue to address). However, if it's not just a modification of child support which must be resolved, but perhaps issues beyond child support like visitation or asset distribution, then Supreme Court is better equipped for these situations. The reason for this is Family Court does not have jurisdiction to rule in asset/property distribution issues - and the court will deal with visitation before a separate Judge from the support issue (as opposed to Supreme Court, where the same judge will rule on both issues). Thus, if one has an issue such as modification/termination of support due to a refusal of visitation rights, then it's better to file the application in Supreme Court.

Finally, if in between times your driver's license has been suspended due to child support arrears, you may additionally file an application to restore your license. You may find the form here: https://www.nycourts.gov/LegacyPDFS/FORMS/familycourt/pdfs/4-22.pdf.

Can I Do Anything If the Other Parent's Downward Modification of Support Petition Is Granted?

If a modification is granted by the court and you disagree with it, then your only option is to appeal that decision. You have the right to oppose the downward modification case. If this is the case, hiring an attorney to assist with the process enables your case to go as smoothly as possible. An experienced attorney will know how to prove your case with the statutory factors involved. These statutory laws include a 15% difference of income, and at least 3 years passing since the order was last modified or originally set. If the non-custodial parent satisfies these standards, this reopens a new child support calculation process. In this case, you have just as much right as the non-custodial parent does to present both testimony and evidence in support of a revised calculation. In this circumstance, hiring an adept child support attorney to defend your case is a crucial step in your appeal process. If your case is lost, then you would follow the same appeals procedure (which is in Family Court), where you would file an objection appeal within 30 days. If it's in the Supreme Court, you must also file a notice of appeal within 30 days (or 35 days if the decision was mailed).

What Is an Upward Modification Of Support In New York?

An upward modification of support is asking the court to raise the amount of child support, which is almost always done by the custodial parent. The degree of difficulty in getting an upward modification depends on whether a divorce settlement agreement exists and when it was set. If it was set before 2010 (& unless the divorce settlement agreement says otherwise), the standard is an "unanticipated change of circumstances." This means one is extremely *unlikely* to get any change at all for the life of the case. If this was not stated in the settlement, or if your agreement was *not* done before 2010, then the regular modification standards would apply. The regular modification standards would also apply to agreements that do not specifically opt-out of the statutory standard (post-2010 amendment to the law).

Post-2010, any agreement must state whether it is opting out of the statutory standards to modify child support. If your agreement is silent on the issue, then the statutory standards apply. The statutory modification standard are:

- It's been more than three years since the child support was set or last modified
- A change in either parent's income by 15%, or
- Some other substantial changes of circumstances.

If the custodial parent seeking a raise in child support has satisfied one of those standards, the court would rule on the case like a regular child support calculation. As such, the custodial parent would need to submit the mandatory disclosure regarding their basis to raise child support, and the non-custodial parent would likewise have to put in their mandatory disclosure. These are financial disclosure affidavits (link to the form here: https://www.nycourts.gov/LegacyPDFS/FORMS/familycourt/pdfs/4-17.pdf), which include details such as last filed tax returns and pay stubs. Then the court would do a recalculation of the child support and reset the child support in accordance with the statutory standards.

What are other Legitimate Reasons a Court Will Consider an Upward Modification of Support?

There are scenarios where expenses have gone up for the children are contributing factors. Consider a situation where the child support calculation was set when the child was six years old, and now 10 years have gone by and that child is now sixteen years old. If that's the case, presumably teenagers are more expensive than younger kids, and the custodial parent may want a raise in child support. If the support agreement says the custodial parent can't raise child support after 3 years, this is a case where there has been a substantial change of circumstances, which is a legitimate reason for the court to consider upward modification of support.

If this happens, you must prove what your expenses were when child support was originally set, and what your expenses are now. Proving these added expenses involves showing bills and receipts for *both* time periods in order to display the change. In many cases, a financial disclosure affidavit or net worth statement is available from the initial child support agreement, and can be used as evidence proving your past expenses (especially helpful if the support was last set or adjusted many years ago & it's difficult to obtain, say, utility bills from 5+ years ago). If this is not the case, you must prove those original expenses with specific bills and receipts.

Other grounds include if there are multiple children, and the original agreement/order was done on a split custody situation (1 or more children living with each parent) and now the custody arrangement has been altered.

Finally, child support can be adjusted administratively if the order if enforced via the Support Collection Unit. The recipient can initiate a "review" process by the SCU - which will then calculate whether the Consumer Price Index has increased at least 10% since the support was set. If it was, then SCU can simply send a notice to the support obligor notifying him/her the support will automatically increase unless s/he files an "Objection" in court.

If you're the support recipient, simply contact your local Support Collection Unit office to request this review process. The benefit of this for the recipient is s/he will not need to go to court to receive the increase.

If you're the support obligor and receive a notice of the proposed increase - and you disagree with the increase - then act promptly by filing the Objection form with the court: https://www.nycourts.gov/LegacyPDFS/FORMS/familycourt/pdfs/4-19.pdf.

Finally, information regarding the filing of Objections and Rebuttals to the automatic increase may be found at the court's website here: https://www.nycourts.gov/LegacyPDFS/FORMS/familycourt/pdfs/4-SM-2.pdf.

How Do I Apply for an Upward Modification of Support in New York Family Court?

The non-custodial parent would apply for a downward modification by accessing the form here: http://ww2.nycourts.gov/forms/familycourt/childsupport.shtml. After completing this form, it is recommended you consult with a family law attorney to make sure that the form is completed correctly. After doing so, then one should file it via the EDDS system at the family court (link here: https://iappscontent.courts.state.ny.us/NYSCEF/live/edds.htm). If you are filing in the Supreme Court, then you would do it by order to show cause - which is not done in a family court petition.

* * *

How Are Child Support Orders Enforced In New York?

Support orders can be enforced administratively through the Support Collection Unit if the original order was done through that agency. Otherwise, if the support order is being violated, one would need to file an enforcement petition. If that is the only issue that is on the docket such as issues of visitation, custody, property, or assets distributions, one should do this process through the Family Court.

As an option, one may send the parent who is violating the support order a default notice letter - because there may be valid reasons why they are violating their support, and it could be beneficial to know these reasons. Take a scenario where the non-custodial parent changes employers, and they are unaware their child support income garnishment didn't transfer to that new job. In this case, the custodial parent would have wasted their time by filing an enforcement petition because eventually, the second employer would implement a new income garnishment from the Support Collection Unit.

Sometimes simply emailing or mailing a letter to the non-custodial parent to clarify these mishaps can avoid legal time and headache.

Moreover, if the order is not enforced via Support Collection Unit and/or the wages are not yet garnished, one may apply to the Court for issuance of an "income deduction order" (a/k/a "garnishment"). The form for that is here: https://www.nycourts.gov/LegacyPDFS/FORMS/familycourt/pdfs/4-8.pdf.

As another example, let's say the non-custodial parent lost their job, but had a job offer lined up to start within a month - and it was explained to the custodial parent they would receive catch-up payments. If they were able to come to an agreement via negotiating amongst themselves, it would avoid going through the hassle of filling out forms and getting the court involved. A default notice letter is not required, but it can save time and money as well as decrease the gaps in payment. Furthermore, by sending a default notice letter, it sets up the non-custodial parent for an award of counsel fees. Some settlement agreements done in a divorce case will specifically articulate that default notice letters have to be sent if any aspect of the divorce settlement (including child support) agreement is being violated.

If this wasn't done, the non-custodial parent would not automatically get an award of counsel fees - rather they would have to prove an element called a "willful violation" of the support order. If the custodial parent either didn't want to file a default notice letter, or there was an issue that wasn't rectified, then they would file an "enforcement petition", which is a petition that can be found on nycourts.gov by following the link to child support (link here: https://www.nycourts.gov/LegacyPDFS/FORMS/familycourt/pdfs/4-13.pdf).

What Will New York Courts Do If Administrative Remedies Are Not Effective to Enforce A Support Order?

The court can do many things through the violation of a support order. Administrative remedies usually constitute things like the Support Collection Unit attempting to garnish wages, suspended licenses, or bank seizures. If those administrative remedies do not prove successful, then the court has a variety of other options to enforce a support order.

If, for instance, the person changed jobs, they can direct a new income garnishment to be issued. Additionally, if the person lost their job can't find a new one the court now has the power to order them into a jobs program. This (among other things) would certify to the court that they are making an earnest effort to look for work. The Judge can also require the support obligor to affirmatively seek employment and document his/her efforts to the Court.

Another thing that the court can do is issue a money judgment that would accrue 9% interest on the arrears, which is a relatively high-interest rate. This encourages the person who violates their support order to pay the money owed faster by putting it on a series of credit cards. This is because most credit cards do not charge 9% interest, and if they know the support order is charging them 9% interest on their payments, then it makes more fiscal sense to start the payments on a credit card.

In addition to these things, the Family Court also has the ability to put the person in violation of their support payments on probation and or put in jail. There are many different scenarios that can occur when a person goes to jail for a support order violation. They can be put in jail for up to six months consecutively (which is the top penalty), or they could be put in jail for certain days of the week (for example, weekends only). The order would have to be very specific about these terms, and often, if the person did not report to jail on their specified day, then an arrest warrant would go out for them. If this occurs, the person would most likely go to jail for the full six consecutive months.

Consider another situation where a violation petition is filed, and the non-custodial parent rectifies their payments by the time of the trial on the violation case. The court can implement "an undertaking", which is put in place in light of various past violations. If this is the case, they will order that parent to set money aside in an escrow account to ensure that the custodial parent would be able to have access to that account until they are able to get back into court and rectify the issue. The form for an undertaking may be found here: https://www.nycourts.gov/LegacyPDFS/FORMS/familycourt/pdfs/4-5a.pdf.

Can I Appeal a Decision By The Court To Modify or Enforce Child Support In New York?

You can appeal a decision by the court regarding modification or enforcement of child support if it's a final order determining the child support issue. In Family Court, this is done by filing an "objection appeal", which can usually be done physically at the family court. Again, post-pandemic, you have the option to file it by the EDDS system. It is important to know that you only have 30 days to file your objection appeal in Family Court. In Family Court, you would generally need to file an objection brief that lays out the basic facts that you put in to support your petition (the link to the Objection form may be found here: https://www.nycourts.gov/LegacyPDFS/FORMS/familycourt/pdfs/4-7b.pdf). With these facts (that were otherwise put in by the custodial parent), you then make a legal argument as to why you're asserting that the Magistrate made a mistake. It is also important to order transcripts of all the hearing dates in order to make your case by referencing specific statements made during the initial hearings.

The other way to appeal would be if your case was in Supreme Court. In this situation, you would file a notice of appeal. This is a different document than the objection brief done in family court. A notice of appeal is a one-page form (the link to the form for the 2d Dept. may be found here: https://www.nycourts.gov/courts/AD2/forms/noticeofappeal.pdf) that also contains attachments called the "RADI form" and "proof of service", which must both be attached to the underlying order. The actual appellate brief won't be due for months after you file a notice of appeal.

Another thing to be aware of is that the Appellate Court can only look at the actual evidence and testimony entered during the trial, and they cannot consider any new evidence. Consider, for example, the following situation: An upward modification of support is granted, partially because the non-custodial parent put in a poor defense against the modification. In this case, the non-custodial parent could not reargue their case to the Appellate Court.

Anything that should have been argued or put into evidence needs to be done at the trial level. So, when it comes to the appeals process, there is only so much a family law attorney can do to create an appellate brief after an upward modification case has already been lost.

Nevertheless, handling an appeal is outside the scope of this book - which is more intended to address issues at the Supreme Court or Family Court level. One may consult the following practice aid of the Appellate Division, Second department for more general information on filing an appeal: https://www.nycourts.gov/courts/AD2/pdf/Guide%20to%20Practice.pdf.

Appendix A

Custody Timeline

The timeline can include events over the last few years leading up to the custody filing - as well as events which occur as the case is proceeding. The "link to evidence" would be a reference to a particular document which may serve to corroborate the event - a picture, a text/e-mail, a video, another witness, etc. You may also wish to organize it topically rather than by date (e.g., "scheduling difficulties," "hostile/denigrating attitudes," etc.). You can also include dates/times when you were attempting to reach the child(ren) while they were with the other parent & were unable to. Examples of evidence: texts, e-mails, police report, witnesses, medical/school records, etc. When preparing trial exhibits, these need to be specified & linked to the individual events one wishes to present testimony on.

Date	Key Event	Link to Evidence

APPENDIX B

Relocation Factor Chart

Factors	Mother	Father
Each parent's reasons for seeking or opposing the		
The quality of the relationships between the child and the custodial and noncustodial parents		
The impact of the move on the quantity and quality of the child's future contact with the noncustodial parent		

The degree to which the custodial parent's and child's life may be enhanced economically, emotionally and educationally by the move		
The feasibility of preserving the relationship between the noncustodial parent and child through suitable visitation		
Any other factors/facts which client thinks is relevant for the court either		

APPENDIX C

Job search diary

You must write a contact name, address and date for every place where you looked for work[31] and/or submitted a job application or resume – you may include contacts with potential employers either in-person, or via phone/E-mail. Please make additional copies of this diary as are needed to supply the complete list of every single potential employer you had contact with. Please attach copies of all correspondence to/from each potential employer and print-outs from website submissions, as well as notes of all phone contact (including a fair summary of each conversation).

---

[31] Non-exhaustive list of places to look for work in the greater NYC area are (besides the major, national job sites): https://humanresources.westchestergov.com/, Westchester/Bronx Co. Dept. of Labor (One-Stop Career Center: www.labor.ny.gov/workforcenypartners/osview.asp), https://www.westchesterjobs.com/, www.cs.ny.gov/jobseeker, www.usajobs.gov, www.southbronx.jobcorps.gov/home.aspx, https://www1.nyc.gov/jobs/index.page.

Date:

Employer Name:

Address/Phone Number:

Contact Person:

Results:

Date:

Employer Name:

Address/Phone Number:

Contact Person:

Results:

Date:

Employer Name:

Address/Phone Number:

Contact Person:

Results:

Date:

Employer Name:

Address/Phone Number:

Contact Person:

Results:

Date:

Employer Name:

Address/Phone Number:

Contact Person:

Results:

Date:

Employer Name:

Address/Phone Number:

Contact Person:

Results:

About The Author

David Bliven graduated with honors from Syracuse University in 1993 with a B.A. in Sociology. He went on to serve as a statistician with the NYS Commission on City Court Judicial Reallocation with the Office of the Deputy Chief Administrative Judge. He then attended New York Law School where he graduated in 1997 with honors and ranked within the top 15% of his class.

Shortly after graduating, he served as a prosecutor for nearly 3 years with the NYC Administration for Children's Services. While at ACS he prosecuted child support, child abuse & neglect and foster care cases on behalf of the City of New York.

After leaving the prosecutor position, Mr. Bliven opened his present practice in 2000. His practice is currently devoted 100% to Divorce & Family Court cases.

Mr. Bliven has an "AV" rating from Martindale-Hubbell (the highest possible rating in both Legal Ability & Ethical Standards), a perfect 10.0 rating from Avvo ("Superb" rating) and is listed in the "Super Lawyers" directory by Thompson Reuters (a distinction given to less than 5% of all attorneys in each field of practice). He is also a "Certified Financial Litigator" and was honored as a "Super Lawyer" for the NY Metro & Westchester area by *Westchester Magazine* in their October, 2019 issue.

Mr. Bliven has authored the books "Navigating Your New York Divorce Case, "Navigating Your New York Family Court Case" and "Navigating Your New York High Net Worth Divorce Case." His articles have been published in the New York Law Journal, Nolo.com and Westchester Lawyer Magazine.

TESTIMONIALS

- Anonymous: "During a time, when it seemed as my life was about to fall apart, Mr. Bliven was there to make sure I was protected. Mr. Bliven was there to make sure every "T" was crossed and every "I" was dotted. He made sure I was entitled to my fair share. When children are involved in a divorce, I wanted to make sure they were taken care of for the foreseeable future. Mr. Bliven made it his duty to fight for me when he felt I deserved more retribution. He fought tooth and nail for the needs of my children as well as for me. During a time when things looked bleak, Mr. Bliven made sure my legal and financial needs are taken care of. When beginning this venture, I was scared that I would walk off of this with only my "shirt", but Mr. Bliven made it his job to make sure I was able to resume my life without looking back. I want to thank Mr. Bliven and I would recommend him to anyone who is and is thinking about filing for a divorce."

- Jonathan: "Mr. Bliven came very highly recommended to me by a friend who used to practice family law and had transitioned into other areas of legal practice. I was not disappointed. Mr. Bliven was thoroughly knowledgeable and highly attentive as he helped me smoothly resolve complex child support matters involving international issues of competing jurisdictions. Having had a number of attorneys in the course of my divorce and child custody/support matters over the last 18 years, I believe I am experienced to know that Mr. Bliven is a top family law expert."

- Lou: "Mr. Bliven represented me in a child support case. I was very pleased with the services provided by Mr. Bliven. He is professional, courteous, and knows his stuff! I am completely gratified with the outcome of my case. Thanks to Mr. Bliven's knowledge of family law. Mr. Bliven kept me up to date on all matters pertaining to my case and his billing is fair and accurate for the work he puts into the case. I would certainly recommend him to anyone that is seeking a topnotch lawyer in the area family court."

- Teri Colon: "Although I have not met with Mr. Bliven yet. I contacted his office on a Friday of a Holiday Weekend. His office's response was immediate and I was treated with respect as if I was already a client. His staff took the time to email me immediately and when I called I was given an appointment that accommodates my schedule. Custody matters are very sensitive and clients can be emotional. It was a relief to speak with someone who was not only professional and courtesy, but also showed genuine concern. I look forward to my consultation with Mr. Bliven."

- Ariane: "Mr. Bliven was knowledgeable, informative, and an incredible strategist. He used all of my legal rights to defend me in my case and was extremely professional to work with. I can't thank him enough for his ability to use our rights as law-abiding citizens and to get the job done. David consulted with me on all motions before revealing them to the court or to any other parties. For this I thank him and am grateful for his diligence in representation."

- Gregg: "Although I subscribe to a legal plan through my union (I'm a teacher), I decided to retain Mr. Bliven based on our initial consultation. He seemed much better versed than the less expensive "plan" attorney I spoke to in the child support matter I brought to him. Mr. Bliven scanned the paperwork I brought with me to the consultation and immediately developed a strategy using various points of law. Mr. Bliven kept in constant contact with me and "cc'd" me on all correspondence he and my ex-wife's attorney had via email or hard-copy. Mr. Bliven's courtroom demeanor was just as I had hoped it would be; vocal and on point. Ultimately, my ex-wife and I reached a fair compromise that did not follow the default percentages NY State dictates. I would definitely retain again should the need arise."

- A Satisfied Client: "Navigating family court for personal reasons can be quite intimidating, even for folks who have interfaced with court officers and judges for professional purposes. That said, Bliven was nothing short of extremely knowledgeable, courteous and very attuned with the emotional experience that comes with the process. I highly recommend Bliven if you are seeking consultation and representation with a child support and/or custody case!"

****

More Testimonials may be found on David Bliven's website (http://www.blivenlaw.net/Testimonials.shtml) and at Avvo (https://www.avvo.com/attorneys/10463-ny-david-bliven-952796.html#client_reviews).

*　　*　　*　　*

If you appreciated the information given to you in this book, Mr. Bliven would appreciate a review of the book on Amazon and/or a Google review:

https://g.page/law-offices-of-david-bliven-933/review?rc

INDEX

S

T

U

V

W

NOTES